Nice and concise.

Naomi Moore-
Rockville, MD

Crazy Little Shorts gives you a great insight on the ever changing tax laws that ordinary people do not keep up with. It helps give you the knowledge you need to make some early decisions before getting your taxes done.

Todd Nicholas-
Semmes, AL

Informative and good overview.

R.C. Roux-
Mobile, AL

Crazy Little Shorts For These Taxing Times is a terrific resource that should be on everyone's desk. I love the cover—so Non-CPAish.

Steve Clark-
Navarre, FL

Great job! Lots of good info.

Dan Detman-
Daphne, AL

I like Richard's book. Good information in a digest form so busy people like me can actually get some good nuggets without having to read a 550 page boring technical report!!

John H. Curry, CLU, ChFC, AEP, MSFS, CSA, CLTC-
Tallahassee, FL

Mr. Lindsey's book was great… My husband and I both enjoyed the vast knowledge it gave us. Thanks for putting out there things we had no clue about.

Anita Motykiewicz-
Mobile, AL

Very Good.

Jane Ann Lance-
Mobile, AL

I actually enjoyed reading *Crazy Little Shorts For These Taxing Times*. It was very concise, informative and quite easy to read. I found it helpful for my tax year and for future tax planning. That's one of the reasons I have had my taxes prepared by Richard for many years.

Debbie Gautreaux-
Mobile, AL

Crazy Little Shorts
For These Taxing Times

48 Tax Shorts for Every Day Planning

Richard A. Lindsey, CPA

Published by :
Zevac & Lindsey, L.L.C.
1050 Hillcrest Rd., Ste A
Mobile, AL 36695
(251) 633-4070—phone
(251) 633-4071—fax
www.ZevacLindsey.com

Compiled and edited by Richard A. Lindsey, CPA, 2010, Revised 2011

tax shorts *n.* (1) Not as long as normal for its kind (2) A brief introduction to a tax topic

Confessions of a CPA

Who is Richard Lindsey? Why should you listen to me?

My name is Richard Lindsey and I have a crazy idea for you. Learn just enough about taxes to ask the right questions.

You might be wondering why I'm in a straight jacket and why you should listen to a crazy idea from a guy like me. The answers are amazingly simple: (a) to get noticed, and (b) because I have 20 years experience as a CPA and 15 years before that in the family business. I've seen good years and lean years. There have been times when I sought professional help one year and then tried to copy it on my own the next, totally unaware of the changes that had occurred in the world around me. Because I hadn't kept up, I didn't even know the right questions to ask. I didn't realize at the time that professional help could have actually <u>saved</u> me money. —No, professional help is not just for the rich, they just already know it pays for itself.

It's been said that a little knowledge is a dangerous thing. However if you take a tiny little kernel of knowledge, plant it, water and nurture it with professional help, it can grow into a beautiful thing.

Whether you're training for a marathon, landing the job of your dreams or closing a sale, you're not going to excel without being well prepared and fully informed.

Well, the same holds true when managing and preparing your taxes.

Waiting until April 15th to put your financial house in order is a straight path to paying higher taxes. To manage your taxes and minimize your tax bill, you need to know the rules of the game, which are constantly changing, and you want to take advantage of year-round tax-planning opportunities.

The good news is that it's not too late to get started. This little book is not intended to make you a tax expert. It's intended to give you little kernels of knowledge. Few topics in this book are given little more than an introduction. Read the book through. It won't take you more than a few minutes. When you find something that might be applicable in your life, plant it in your mind by marking the page. Water and nurture it by consulting with your tax advisor. Beware: tax preparer does not equal tax advisor. Anyone with a pencil or a computer can be a tax preparer. No licensing, training or education required.

Planning and timing are critical, and tax issues will change throughout the year. Every year brings many tax-related changes as Congress considers estate-tax changes, healthcare reform and other important legislation.

You should therefore regularly monitor your financial situation and consult with your tax advisor if you believe you may be affected by any changes in tax law. By taking the necessary, responsive steps as soon as the need arises, rather than delaying action until the end of the year, you can better protect your family's financial interests.

READ ON ⇒

Contents

SPECIAL NOTE:

Due date of return. File Form 1040, 1040A, or 1040EZ by April 17, 2012. The due date is April 17, instead of April 15, because April 15 is a Sunday and April 16 is the Emancipation Day holiday in the District of Columbia

2011 Tax Rates

The tax rates remain the same as last year. The six tax brackets are 10%, 15%, 25%, 28%, 33% and 35%. The tax rates are scheduled to remain the same for 2011 and 2012. Be aware of the coming changes. President Obama's current plan is to raise the tax rates to the higher 2001 levels.

Filing Status

There are five categories of filing status: single, married filing jointly, married filing separately, head of household and qualifying widow(er). The primary factor impacting your filing status is whether you are married or not.

If you are married, you and your spouse must decide whether to file jointly or separately. In most cases, you'll pay lower taxes if you file jointly. Also, be aware that your choice may impact your state income-tax calculation, as many states require consistency with federal tax-return filings.

If you are not married, you can use the single filing status or the head of household filing status if you have a dependent. Heads of household pay a significantly lower tax rate than singles, but to qualify you must meet the requirements for supporting at least one other dependent.

If you are a qualifying widow(er), you may use the joint tax rates for two years following the year of death of your spouse, as long as (1) you have a qualifying dependent, (2) you provide more than half the cost of keeping up a home for you and your dependent, and (3) you did not remarry.

If more than one filing status applies to you, you may want to choose the one that results in the lowest tax obligation. Here's a planning hint: In a two-wage earner family where one might have been laid off for a significant part of the year, you may want to consider whether married filing separately reduces your overall federal tax liability.

Other circumstances include when one spouse has high unreimbursed medical expenses or a significant amount of miscellaneous itemized deductions. The only way to be sure is to compute your taxes both ways, a task easily performed by most tax-preparation software packages.

Alternative Minimum Tax (AMT) Patch

In addition to the regular income tax, more and more taxpayers are finding themselves subject to the Alternative Minimum Tax (AMT). The AMT, which was created by the Tax Reform Act of 1969, was designed to ensure equitable taxes are paid by higher-income taxpayers. As the AMT was not indexed for inflation, tax-payers are increasingly finding themselves affected.

Some of the items that can trigger the AMT include a higher-than-average number of dependency exemptions, large deductions for state and local income taxes, higher real estate taxes, high miscellaneous itemized deductions, and high medical expenses.

AMT Exemption Amounts

The Alternative Minimum Tax exemption amounts for 2010 are $47,450 for a single individual and $72,450 for married individuals filing a joint return. For 2011, these exemption amounts increase to $48,450 for a single individual and $74,450 for married individuals filing a joint return.

Unfortunately, the AMT defies most traditional tax-planning strategies. If you've been close to the threshold, you'll need to consult with your CPA for specific advice on how the AMT may affect you.

Standard Deduction

Every year, the IRS adjusts the standard deduction to account for inflation. For 2010, the standard deduction is $5,700 for single filers or married couples filing separately, and it jumps to $11,400 for married couples filing jointly and for qualifying widow(er)s. It's $8,400 for head-of-household filers.

For 2011, the standard deduction is $5,800 for single filers and married couples filing separately, $11,600 for married couples filing jointly and qualifying widow(er)s, and $8,500 for head-of-household filers.

Standard Deduction Additions

Taxpayers age 65 and older, and/or blind, receive an additional standard deduction of $1,150, and $1,450 if the individual is also unmarried and does not have a surviving spouse.

An individual who is both, age 65 or older and blind, may take two additional standard deductions. Married taxpayers filing jointly, both of whom are age 65 or older and blind, would be able to claim four additional standard deduction amounts.

Although not true for Alabama, if you take a standard deduction for federal purposes some states may require you to file your state return also taking the standard deduction. Conversely, if you itemize for federal purposes you will have to itemize for state purposes. This is important because some federal deductions are not allowed as a state deduction, such as your state income tax.

Itemizing Deductions

An alternative to claiming the standard deduction is itemizing your deductions. To determine the best strategy for you, total all of your deductions. In general, if your total allowable itemized deductions are more than the standard deduction, then by all means, itemize. It will save you money. In addition, if you are subject to the AMT you need to consider whether you want to bunch your deductions in any one year.

Itemized deductions include healthcare costs not reimbursed by insurance, health insurance premiums and long-term care insurance premiums, specific state and local taxes, mortgage interest, charitable contributions, and other miscellaneous items such as tax-return preparation fees, investment advisory fees and unreimbursed employee business expenses. For 2010 and 2011, you may also choose to deduct sales taxes paid if it exceeds your state income tax. Tables for this are provided in the IRS instructions.

The limit on itemized deductions for high-income taxpayers is completely phased out for 2010, 2011, and 2012. Higher-income taxpayers are not required to reduce the amount of their itemized deduction when their AGI exceeds certain threshold amounts.

Here's another tip: If you find you're getting close to exceeding the standard deduction limit, try bunching your tax breaks every other year. This allows you to claim the standard deduction one year, but itemize the next, but it also allows you to plan for the maximum tax benefit.

Also, since itemized deductions are a factor in determining if you're subject to the AMT, some pre-planning might help if you are in this situation.

Charitable Deductions

Making charitable contributions can instill a feeling of goodwill and tax laws have been created to recognize your philanthropic efforts. Donations you make by cash, check or credit card to qualified charitable institutions are deductible up to 50% of your AGI, if you itemize your deductions. If your donations exceed 50%, you can carry the excess forward for up to five years.

Remember to obtain and keep a record to substantiate all donations. Substantiating documents range from a cancelled check and credit card statement to a W-2 form and a written statement from the organization. The type and extent of documentation is usually determined by the amount of the donation.

There are other ways of sharing your good fortune that also deliver tax benefits.

Donating appreciated assets that qualify for the long-term capital gains treatment can actually do more to cut your tax bill. When you give appreciated long-term securities to a non-profit, you deduct the full market value of the asset at the time of the donation and you avoid paying capital gains tax on the appreciation. Be sure to follow substantiation requirements.

Taxpayers can only deduct a charitable donation of $250 or more if they have a statement from the charitable organization showing the amount of money contributed and a description (but not value) of any property donated and whether the organization did or did not give the taxpayer any goods or services in return for the contribution.

A tax deduction for clothing and household items is allowed if the items are in good condition and you can show comparable values for the item.

Dividends

Dividend income received by an individual shareholder from a domestic or qualified foreign company is taxed at a top rate of 15% and at just 0% for taxpayers in the 10% or 15% tax brackets for 2010, 2011 and 2012. However, these tax rates are subject to review, so watch for media reports on the topic and seek council from your CPA as changes occur.

It's important to keep in mind that to receive a dividend that qualifies for the lower tax rate, you must buy the stock at least one day before the ex-dividend date and hold that stock for at least 60 more days. The ex-dividend date is the last date on which shareholders of record are entitled to receive the upcoming dividend. Essentially, what this means is that if you owned shares for only a short time around the ex-dividend date, your dividend income will be taxed as ordinary income and will not be eligible for the 15% rate.

Here's another caveat: not all income payments that are called dividends are qualified dividends in the true "taxed at 15%" sense. For example, the money you earn on savings accounts, certificates of deposit and money market funds is sometimes referred to as dividends, but is actually interest and is taxed as ordinary income.

In any case, you should never let tax considerations alone drive your investment decisions. Be sure that your overall financial objectives guide your investment strategies.

Capital Gains Tax

The maximum tax rate on net long-term capital gains is 15% for 2010, 2011 and 2012. If you're in the 10% or 15% tax brackets, your net long-term capital gains rate is zero, and you will not be taxed for 2010, 2011 and 2012. To qualify for long-term tax treatment, an asset must be held for more than one year before it is sold. For coins, art and other collectibles held for more than one year, the maximum capital gains tax rate is 28%.

Capital gains on investments held for one year or less are taxed at regular income tax rates.

Offset Capital Gains with Losses

When it comes to investment decisions, knowing when to make a move is critical. Then there are times, such as those we are experiencing today, where many of our conventional ideas about investing are dramatically challenged.

If you have any capital gains, you can reduce your taxes by offsetting your gains against sales of investments that resulted in losses. If your capital losses exceed your capital gains, you can deduct up to $3,000 in net capital losses against ordinary income ($1,500 if married filing separately) or your total net loss as shown in 1040 Schedule D, *Capital Gains and Losses*, whichever is less.

Excess losses that you could not deduct may be carried forward to future years and can be used to offset future gains. This is in addition to being able to deduct up to $3,000 in future years. It is very important to keep track of these unused losses and whether they are short-term or long-term losses.

Keep in mind that an investment sold at a loss need not be gone forever. If you believe it was a good long-term investment, you can buy it back. Just be sure to wait at least 31 days after the sale. Otherwise you'll get caught up in the wash sale rule.

This rule disallows losses on securities sold if substantially identical securities are bought within 30 days before or after the loss sale, although the definition of "substantially identical" does provide some flexibility.

The current capital gains rates expire after 2012 and there has been significant discussion that the rates may be increased for taxpayers above certain income levels.

Remember to work with a qualified investment professional.

Shifting Income

There are some long-term strategies you can employ to reduce your taxes on investment income for college savings. As with all investment strategies, they have to be right for you and appropriate for the economic environment. The current economy makes some of these strategies more or less beneficial, depending on your circumstances. I highly recommend that you first check with a financial advisor.

Now, let's begin with strategies for how parents can save on taxes. Shifting income to a child in a lower tax bracket was a popular strategy. The Kiddie Tax may have a place in your overall tax plan.

A child can earn investment income up to $950 tax free. The next $950 is taxed at the child's rate, which for dividends and capital gains, can be as low as 0%. Any investment income over $1,900 will be taxed at your own top rate. It won't pay to shift a significant amount of income to a child falling under the Kiddie Tax rules, but transferring a few income-producing assets to a child might still lower your overall tax bill.

And, it's important to know that shifting income to your child will also reduce the adjusted gross income on your personal return, which may mean that you'll lose less of your itemized deductions and personal exemptions. Lowering your AGI may also make you eligible for other tax benefits.

Also, be sure to consider the gift tax when shifting assets. For 2010 and 2011, you generally can give a gift to a child, or anyone else, valued up to $13,000 each without being subject to the gift tax. Spouses who agree to split their gifts may transfer a total of $26,000 per donee free of gift tax. The exclusion is allowed only for cash gifts or present interest in property.

Hiring Your Children

If you're a sole proprietor, you can shift income by hiring your children to help in your business. In addition to providing valuable work experience for your child, this arrangement offers significant tax savings to the business. As long as the work your children do is legitimate, you follow all the rules and they receive reasonable wages, you can deduct their wages as a business expense and shift the money to your children in lower tax brackets.

As an added bonus, if your son or daughter is under 18, you don't have to pay Social Security or Medicare taxes on the wages you pay. Because of the standard deduction, in 2010, the first $5,700 earned by each child is not taxed. In 2011, the first $5,800 earned by each child will be non-taxable. Also, since it's earned income, it isn't subject to the Kiddie Tax. Just be sure to file W-2 forms and other necessary tax forms for the child.

Newly Married

Remember, you and your sweetie might need to adjust your withholdings from work.

If you get a big tax refund each year, it doesn't mean that you are getting a bonus from the government. You overpaid your taxes from the previous year, and they are just sending back your overpayment. That's a bad idea. You just let the government use your money interest-free for one year. Make that money work for you!

Make sure that both of you adjust your withholdings at work. When you pay your taxes each year, you want to come as close to zero as possible (meaning you don't owe the government, and they don't owe you). This is true for singles and married couples.

If you have recently gotten married here are some other tips to help you avoid stress at tax time.

1. **Notify the Social Security Administration**. Report any name change to the Social Security Administration, so your name and SSN will match when you file your next tax return. Informing the SSA of a name change is quite simple. File a Form SS-5, Application for a Social Security card at your local SSA office. The form is available on SSA's website at www.socialsecurity.gov, by calling (800) 772-1213 or at local offices.
2. **Notify the IRS.** If you have a new address you should notify the IRS by sending Form 8822, Change of Address. You may download Form 8822 from the IRS website www.irs.gov, or order it by calling (800) TAX-FORM (800-829-3676).
3. **Notify the U.S. Postal Service.** You should also notify the U.S. Postal Service when you move, so it can forward any IRS correspondence.
4. **Notify Your Employer.** Report any name and address changes to your employer(s) to ensure receipt of your Form W-2, Wage and Tax Statement after the end of the year.

New Baby

In order to claim your new child as a dependent on your tax return, the first thing you need to do is get your new bundle of joy a Social Security number. If you don't, you'll delay the process. You can request a Social Security card at the hospital when you apply for a birth certificate.

Single Parent

If you're a single parent, you may be able to file your returns as head of household rather than single. The advantage? You get a bigger standard deduction, and you'll fit into a better tax bracket. In order to be considered head of household, you must pay more than half the cost of providing a home for a qualifying person (your child).

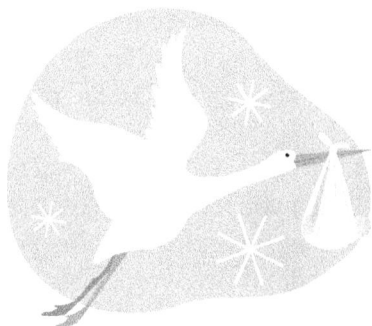

Child Tax Credit

For 2010, 2011 and 2012, the Child Tax Credit is worth $1,000 for each qualifying child who is under age 17 at the end of the calendar year and who qualifies as a dependent—your son, daughter, adopted child, step child or eligible foster child, brother, sister, step brother, step sister, or a descendant of any of these individuals. The child must also be a U.S. citizen or resident. The Child Tax Credit is in addition to the child's dependency exemption.

That means if you have three children, the child credit can potentially reduce your tax bill by $3,000. Keep in mind that the $1,000 credit remains in effect through 2012, starting in 2013 it will decrease to $500 per qualifying child.

For 2010, the child credit begins to phase out when modified AGI exceeds $110,000 for married couples filing jointly, $55,000 for married taxpayers filing separately, and $75,000 for single filers, heads of households and qualified widow(er)s. The credit is reduced by $50 for each $1,000, or fraction thereof, of modified AGI above these thresholds.

Beginning in 2013, the refundable component of the credit applies only for families with three or more children subject to a reduction for taxpayers with AMT liability.

Some lower-income households may receive a refund under the Enhanced or Additional Child Tax Credit even if they do not owe any tax. Under the new law, the additional credit is refundable to the extent of 15% of your earned income in excess of $3,000.

Dependent Care Credit

Working parents know how expensive child care can be. The Dependent Care Tax Credit aims to ease some of the burden. Basically, the credit works like this: If, in order to work or look for work, you pay someone to care for a dependent under age 13 who you also claim as a dependent, you may be eligible for a tax credit of up to $2,100. The credit is a percentage of qualifying expenses that range between 20% and 35%. You must have earned income to receive the credit and if married, file a joint return.

For 2010, the dollar limit on the expenses toward which you can apply the credit percentage is $3,000 for the care of one dependent and $6,000 for two or more. The percentage of the expenses you can take as a credit depends on your AGI. These dollar limits must be reduced by the amount of any dependent-care benefits provided by your employer, excluded from your income.

Take note that the Dependent Care Tax Credit isn't restricted to child-related care costs. If you pay someone to look after an incapacitated dependent of any age, such as a parent or disabled family member (for example a spouse who is physically or mentally incapable of self-care), you may be eligible for this tax break.

You will need documentation to claim the Dependent Care Tax Credit, which specifies an invoice from the provider that includes the name of the care provider, address and employer identification number.

Adoption Credit

There is good news for people who are planning to adopt a child. Two tax benefits offset the escalating expenses of adopting an eligible child.

In 2009, the maximum adoption credit rose to $12,150 per child. Parents who work for companies with an Adoption Assistance Program can receive up to a $12,150 reimbursement from their employer for adoption expenses without paying taxes on that benefit.

This benefit phases out for modified AGIs between $185,210 and $225,210. The credit is completely phased-out at $225,210.

For 2010 and 2011, the adoption credit amount is increased and the credit is refundable. In 2010 the credit amount is $13,170 and for 2011 increases to $13,360. The adoption credit will then become non-refundable and the maximum amount will revert back to $5,000 and $6,000 in the case of a special needs child. The phase out range will be $75,000 to $115,000 and the AMT amounts will be adjusted according to inflation.

When you adopt a child with special needs, you are allowed to claim these benefits regardless of actual expenses paid or incurred in the year the adoption becomes final. You are assumed to have incurred the maximum amount of qualifying expenses and may claim the full credit.

When adopting a child from within the United States, the family is permitted to take the credit in the year following the year where the actual expense was incurred. These expenses are deductible even if the adoption ultimately is not completed. This is different from how adoption expenses are treated if the child is from outside the United States.

Where a foreign adoption is involved, the family may not deduct any expenses until the adoption is final, which considering the time and uncertainty of a foreign adoption, places an added burden on the family financing the cost of the adoption. Clearly, in this situation, the longer the adoption process, the more expenses are incurred, none of which are deductible until the adoption is finalized.

Earned Income Credit

Although the Earned Income Credit (EIC) applies to eligible low-wage taxpayers without children, those with children receive the largest benefit. EIC is subtracted directly from the amount of tax you owe. Even if you do not owe any tax to the IRS on your tax return, you might still get some money back. However, you must have earned income—as an employee or self-employed.

On 2010 returns, the maximum credit can be as much as $5,666 for workers supporting three or more qualifying children. A worker with one qualifying child can receive a credit worth up to $3,050 and a worker with two qualifying children can receive a credit worth up to $5,036. For an eligible worker with no qualifying children, the credit drops to $457.

For 2011, the maximum credit amounts are $3,094, $5,112, $5,751 and $464 respectively.

You can include tax-free combat pay as earned income for EIC purposes.

The credit is phased out as AGI increases. Keep in mind also that taxpayers with unearned income such as interest and dividends of more than $3,100 are not eligible for EIC.

U.S. Savings Bonds

Generally, investors who redeem qualified U.S. Savings bonds to pay for qualified higher-education expenses may exclude the interest redeemed from gross income. The exclusion applies to series EE bonds issued after 1989 or series I bonds.

If the interest from the redeemed bond exceeds the amount of qualified education expenses paid, then the exclusion is limited to a fraction of the redeemed amount. The fraction equals the amount of qualified education expenses paid during the tax year over the aggregate proceeds of qualified U.S. Savings bonds redeemed during the tax year.

For 2010, the amount of your interest exclusion is phased out if your filing status is married filing jointly or qualifying widow(er) and your modified AGI is between $105,000 and $135,000. At a modified AGI of $135,000, the exclusion is zero. For single and head of household filers, your interest exclusion is phased out if your modified AGI is between $70,100 and $85,100. You cannot take the exclusion if your modified AGI is $85,100.

For 2011, the amount of your interest exclusion is phased out if your filing status is married filing jointly or qualified widow(er) and your modified AGI is between $106,650 and $136,650. At a modified AGI of $136,650, the exclusion is zero. For single and head of household filers, your interest exclusion is phased out if your modified AGI is between $71,100 and $86,100. You cannot take the exclusion if your modified AGI is $86,100.

Prepaid Tuition Plans

Many states have instituted savings plans substantially similar to the Section 529 Plans that propose to create a prepaid tuition account for a student in that state. The amount contributed will depend on when the plan is begun and the child's age. States have created actuarial tables that they believe will result in a fully funded tuition based on a schedule of deposits and investment-return rates.

The advantage of these plans is that they guarantee tuition costs will be covered. However, they do not guarantee admissions, and they do not cover room and board and the cost of books. These expenses would have to be funded separately. The plans will provide assistance if the student decides not to attend an in-state school; however, it may not cover the full tuition costs of these schools.

You are not restricted to using the savings plans of your state and can use any state's plan. The Internet is an invaluable research tool. However, if you select another state's plan, you may lose a state tax deduction that some states offer to residents who use their state's prepaid or 529 Plans.

In general, the tax treatment of these prepaid tuition plans is similar to section 529 Plan rules.

529 Plans

529 Plans give parents and other family members a tax-advantaged way to save money for college expenses. While there is no tax deduction available on contributions to the plan, the money in the plan grows tax free and no tax is due on withdrawals if the distribution is used to pay for qualified higher-education expenses such as tuition, room and board, books, supplies, and most recently, computers and related peripheral equipment and software.

The 529 Plan is especially valuable as a vehicle for gifts from family members, especially grandparents.

American Opportunity Tax Credit

Many parents and college students will be able to offset the cost of college over the next two years under the new American Opportunity Tax Credit. This tax credit is part of the American Recovery and Reinvestment Act of 2009.

- This credit, which expands and renames the existing Hope Credit, can be claimed for qualified tuition and related expenses that you pay for higher education in 2010, 2011 and 2012. Qualified tuition and related expenses include tuition, related fees, books and other required course materials.
- The credit is equal to 100 percent of the first $2,000 spent and 25 percent of the next $2,000 per student each year. Therefore, the full $2,500 credit may be available to a taxpayer who pays $4,000 or more in qualifying expenses for an eligible student.
- The full credit is generally available to eligible taxpayers who make less than $80,000 or $160,000 for married couples filing a joint return. The credit is gradually reduced, however, for taxpayers with incomes above these levels.
- Forty percent of the credit is refundable, so even those who owe no tax can get up to $1,000 of the credit for each eligible student as cash back.
- The credit can be claimed for qualified expenses paid for any of the first four years of post-secondary education.
- You cannot claim the tuition and fees tax deduction in the same year that you claim the American Opportunity Tax Credit or the Lifetime Learning Credit. You must choose to either take the credit or the deduction, which ever is more beneficial for you.

Lifetime Learning Credit

The Lifetime Learning Credit (LLC) provides a credit of up to $2,000 per year. As its name suggests, the LLC can be used by anyone for undergraduate, graduate and professional degree courses, and it can be claimed for every year that you qualify to receive it.

Unlike the American Opportunity Tax Credit that applies to each student, the LLC applies to each taxpayer and courses taken do not need to be toward a recognized educational credential. Expenses paid with respect to a student for whom the American Opportunity Credit is claimed are not eligible for the LLC.

In 2010, the amount of your LLC is phased out if your modified AGI is between $50,000 and $60,000 ($100,000 and $120,000 if you file a joint return). You cannot claim a LLC if your modified AGI is $60,000 or more ($120,000 or more if you file a joint return).

In 2011, the amount of your LLC is phased out if your modified AGI is between $51,000 and $61,000 ($102,000 and $122,000 if you file a joint return). You cannot claim a LLC if your modified AGI is $61,000 or more ($122,000 or more if you file a joint return).

The lifetime learning credit can not be taken by married taxpayers who file separate returns.

Higher Education Tuition Deduction

You can claim a deduction—up to $2,000 or $4,000—as an adjustment to gross income for expenses (tuition, fees and books) that you paid for higher education at an eligible educational institution.

The deduction applies to you, your spouse and any dependents who you claimed as an exemption. However, to claim the $4,000 deduction, your modified AGI cannot be greater than $65,000 ($130,000 if married filing jointly). For the $2,000 deduction, your modified AGI does not exceed $80,000 ($160,000, if married filing jointly).

The deduction is barred if your filing status is married filing separately or if you claimed an education credit such as the American Opportunity Tax Credit or Lifetime Learning Credit.

Student Loan Interest

If you're paying off student loans, you'll be happy to know that the rules for deducting student loan interest remain liberal. Taxpayers can continue to deduct up to $2,500 of the interest paid on a student loan, regardless of how long it takes to repay the loan. And you don't have to itemize in order to take this deduction. However, there is no deduction if you file as married filing separately, if you are claimed as a dependent or if the loan is from a related party or qualified employer plan.

For the 2010 and 2011 tax years, the deduction is phased out for taxpayers with modified AGI between $60,000 and $75,000 ($120,000 and $150,000 for joint returns). You cannot take a deduction if your modified AGI is $75,000 or more ($150,000 or more for joint returns).

Your First Job

Since you're now getting paid, Uncle Sam thinks he should be paid, too. Get used to taxes coming out of your paycheck because it will never stop. But the good news is that you may be able to deduct certain expenses associated with your job, such as relocation costs if you moved over a certain number of miles.

Obama and Congressional Republicans enacted, for 2011, a temporary, one year reduction in FICA payroll tax. The normal employee rate of 6.2 percent is reduced to 4.2 percent. The rate for self-employed individuals is reduced from 12.4 percent to 10.4 percent.

Making Work Pay Credit

You would think a tax break should be simple. However, more than 15 million taxpayers could unexpectedly owe taxes when they file their federal income tax returns according to a Treasury Department inspector general report issued late 2009. The government was, apparently, too generous with their Making Work Pay tax credit.

The taxpayers most vulnerable include those who have more than one job, couples where both spouses work, and those who receive Social Security benefits while working. The tax credit, which is supposed to pay individuals up to $400 and couples up to $800 (6.2% of earnings), was President Obama's signature tax break in the massive stimulus package enacted February 2009. Most workers received the credit through small increases in their paychecks made available through new withholding tables issued by the Internal Revenue Service (IRS). This tax credit is only available for tax years 2009 and 2010.

The withholding tables, however, do not take into account taxpayers with multiple jobs or marriages in which both people work. They also don't take into account Social Security recipients with jobs that provided taxable income.

The IRS said in a written response that the agency believes the number of people impacted is inflated and that the majority who might be would see "a reduced refund and not an out-of-pocket [tax] liability" come April 15.

Nothing with taxes is ever simple—even when you're supposed to be getting a break.

The Secret Health Care Insurance Deduction

Top Secret

To be a competitive employer and hire talented employees you must offer benefits. This usually includes vacation days, sick days, and often health insurance coverage. With the skyrocketing cost of health insurance it's difficult for many small businesses to offer this.

However, for some employers in Alabama it may have become a little easier in 2009. Back in June 2008, Alabama Governor Bob Riley signed a bill into law that expanded the tax deduction small businesses can take for their employee's health care costs, but almost nobody has written or talked about it since.

The Small Business Health Insurance Premium Deduction Enhancement Bill, which was effective January 1, 2009, allows qualified small business owners to deduct 150 percent of the amount they paid for a qualified employee's health insurance premium from their Alabama state tax return. In addition, the bill also allows qualified employees of those qualified businesses to deduct 150 percent of what they paid for health insurance. So what everyone wants to know is "what qualifies a small business and an employee?"

- **A qualified small business** is one that has less than 25 simultaneously paid full-time employees. No part-time employees are considered. There is no income limitation. This seems pretty straightforward.
- **A qualified employee** is an Alabama resident that works for a qualified business. Also, this employee can not earn more than $50,000 in wages and can have no more than $75,000 of adjusted gross income on the Alabama individual income tax return ($150,000 if married filing joint). This too sounds clear.

It seems fairly uncomplicated from the above descriptions to know who is qualified to take these deductions. However, because the employer can only take the deduction for qualified employees and the qualified employees can only take the deduction if they work for a qualified employer, the tricky part of this deduction is in knowing who is qualified.

For an employee to know the employer qualifies may not be quite as difficult since it is easy to observe if there are less than 25 employees at any given time. However, for employers to know the Alabama adjusted gross income of their individual employees is a little tougher. So what is the solution? The solution lies in communication by both parties.

Employer-Sponsored Plans

Pre-tax contributions to an employer-sponsored savings plan reduces the amount of taxable wages you report on your tax return, making qualified retirement plans an excellent way to cut your tax bill. If you have a 401(k) and you haven't arranged to contribute the maximum, try to increase your contributions before year-end. This is especially important if your employer makes matching contributions, which, in effect, represents free money.

For 2010 and 2011, if you're under age 50, your maximum contribution to a 401(k) plan is $11,500. Taxpayers who are age 50 or older by the end of the year can make an additional $2,500 "catch-up" contribution for that calendar year.

Individual Retirement Accounts (IRAs)

The top annual contribution for traditional or Roth IRAs is $5,000 for 2010 and 2011, provided you have earned income to cover the contribution. If you're age 50 or older by the end of the year, you can make an extra $1,000 "catch up" contribution.

Traditional IRA contributions may be deductible depending on your modified AGI and whether you or your spouse (if filing jointly) is covered by an employer-sponsored retirement plan.

If your spouse does not work for compensation, you can contribute to either a traditional IRA or Roth IRA for your spouse based on your own earnings, with the same dollar limits applying. However, the maximum aggregate that can be contributed to a Roth is reduced by contributions made to other IRAs.

As I mentioned, if you or your spouse participates in a retirement plan at work, your modified AGI may limit the IRA deduction. For joint filers or a qualifying widow(er), who are both active participants in employer-sponsored plans, the 2010 deduction phase-out ranges from $89,000 to $109,000. For tax year 2011, the allowable IRA deduction will be reduced when the modified AGI is between $90,000 and $110,000. For single filers or heads of household, the 2010 and 2011 deduction phases out for incomes between $56,000 and $66,000. For married taxpayers filing separately, no deduction is available once income surpasses $10,000.

If you don't participate in an employer-sponsored plan but your spouse does, the 2010 deduction for your contribution is phased out if your joint modified AGI is more than $167,000 but less than $177,000. However, for tax year 2011, the phase out range will be between $169,000 and $179,000.

With a Roth IRA, contributions are not deductible but you can withdraw them at any time tax free. Investment earnings accumulate on a tax-free basis and may be withdrawn tax free after five years, as long as you meet certain requirements.

For 2010, eligibility to contribute to a Roth IRA is phased out as modified AGI rises from $105,000 to $120,000 if single, head of household or married filing separately and not living with your spouse at any time in 2010; and $167,000 to $177,000 if married filing jointly or qualifying widow(er). Married taxpayers who file separately and lived with their spouse at any time during the year cannot contribute to a Roth IRA if their income is $10,000 or more.

For 2011, the phase out ranges for single individuals and joint filers will run from $107,000 to $122,000 for single, and $169,000 to $179,000 for married joint filers.

You have until the filing deadline of April 15, 2012 to open and contribute to an IRA for 2011. But why wait? The sooner you contribute, the longer your money grows tax deferred or tax free.

To Convert (to a Roth IRA) or Not to Convert? That is the Question

There are a number of advantages for starting a Roth IRA account, the most important being that all the investment earnings grow tax-free, and qualified distributions are tax-free. Additionally, you can continue to make contributions to your Roth after you turn 70 1/2 and are not subject to the required minimum distribution rules. Previously, only individuals who had a modified adjusted gross income (AGI) of less than $100,000 and/or who did not file their return as "married filing separately" could contribute to a Roth IRA, or convert their traditional IRA to a Roth. However, beginning in 2010, everyone, no matter what their income level or filing status, is able to have a Roth IRA. The question that remains is to determine when you should convert, if at all.

Spreading out your tax liability.
A conversion is treated as a taxable distribution, but is not subject to the 10 percent early withdrawal penalty. However, taxpayers who convert to a Roth IRA in 2010 (and 2010, only) have the ability to pay taxes on the converted amount ratably over two years, in 2011 and 2012.

Taking advantage of lower tax rates.
Currently, the income tax rates are at a historic low. But, these rates are scheduled to revert to previously higher levels (and rise further for some taxpayers) after 2012. The Obama administration has proposed extending the lower individual marginal income tax rates, but raising the two highest income tax brackets to 36– and 39.6– percent after 2012. This should be considered in your decision of whether to convert to a Roth in 2010, especially if you expect to be in one of the two highest income tax brackets later.

Wait... There's more →

Undoing the conversion later.

If you convert to a Roth IRA, but later change your mind, you have until Oct. 15 of the year after the year of conversion to undo the transaction and go back to your traditional IRA. For example, if you converted in 2009, you will generally have until October 15, 2010 to re-characterize the transaction. However, to do this you must have filed your individual tax return by the normal filing deadline (April 15, generally), or if you obtained an extension, the extension due date.

For example, if the value of your Roth drastically declines after the conversion, and leaves you essentially with a Roth IRA value that is even less than the tax you paid to convert, this would be a good reason to undo the transaction. Re-characterizing the conversion would undo the tax consequences and therefore you'd get back the tax you paid on the larger amount that was converted to the Roth IRA.

Can you afford the conversion tax?

You will have to pay a conversion tax on the transaction, which can be a significant sum. In spite of all the advantages of a Roth IRA, a conversion is generally advisable if you can readily pay the tax generated in the year of the conversion. If the tax is paid out of a distribution from the converted IRA, that amount is also taxed; and if the distribution counts as an early withdrawal, it is also subject to an additional 10 percent penalty.

New Job

If you are tired of your current job and need a change of scenery, you can possibly deduct some expenses that pertain to job hunting. Examples include: printing and mailing your resume, fees you pay to a job search agency, and even travel expenses if you are looking for work in another state.

There are rules, though. First, the job you're looking for must be in the same line of work as your previous job. Second, and perhaps the most important, job-hunting costs are considered miscellaneous expenses. You can only deduct those kinds of expenses if they exceed 2% of your adjusted gross income.

There are other costs associated with a job change (such as selling your home and moving costs) that may help your tax situation.

Work from Home

Poor money management is one of the top reasons that small businesses go out of business. They don't set aside enough money from profits to pay the government, and they get in trouble with the IRS. The first thing you should do with your profit is to set aside a quarter of the money in a separate business account for taxes.

Always keep your personal and business financial records separate. If you write business expenses out of your personal account, you will severely mess up your records. That's bad enough during any time of the year, but when it comes time to pay your taxes, you'll have an accounting nightmare.

First-Time Homebuyer's Credit

Owning a home has always been part of the American dream. Not only does it create a personal feeling of accomplishment, but it also delivers important tax benefits.

The credit's availability is extended for any individual who serves on qualified extended duty service outside the United States for at least 90 days during the period beginning after December 31, 2008 and ending before May 1, 2010, and, if married, such individual's spouse. In this case, the credit is available for residences purchased before May 1, 2010, and for residences purchased before July 1, 2010, if under a binding contract entered into before May 1, 2010, to close on the purchase before July 1, 2010.

If you purchased your home in 2008 under the original first-time homebuyer's rules, you generally must repay the credit over a 15-year period, which began in 2010. For homes purchased in 2009 and 2010, you must repay the credit only if the home is no longer your principal residence within the 36-month period beginning on the purchase date.

Long-Time Resident Credit

There is also a credit available for long-time residents of the same principal residence purchasing a new residence after November 6, 2009 and before May 1, 2010 (July 1, 2010 if under a binding contract entered into before May 1, 2010 to close on the purchase before July 1, 2010).

The credit is allowed if the taxpayer (and taxpayer's spouse, if married) has owned and used the same residence as a principal residence for any five consecutive-year period during the eight-year period ending on the date of the purchase of a subsequent principal residence.

The credit is equal to the lesser of $6,500 ($3,250 for married tax-payers filing separately) or 10% of the purchase price.

No credit is allowed if the purchase price exceeds $800,000. For purchases after November 6, 2009, the purchaser and the pur-chaser's spouse must be at least 18 by the date of purchase.

Home Deductions

In most cases, you can deduct all of the interest you pay on any loan secured by your home if you itemize your deductions. Interest is deductible on up to $1 million ($500,000 if married filing separately) of home-acquisition loans. These are loans used to buy, build or substantially improve your principal residence or second home, and are secured by that same residence.

Interest on a home-equity loan or line of credit of up to $100,000 ($50,000 if married filing separately) is also deductible. You can also use this deduction for one additional residence that you identify as your second home.

This means you can deduct interest on total home debt up to $1.1 million ($550,000 if married filing separately).

As long as the home-equity loan is secured by your home, it doesn't matter how you spend the proceeds. Home improvements, college tuition, debt consolidation or an exotic vacation—it's up to you. Just be sure you have a plan to pay it back. You will need to itemize your deductions on Schedule A in order to take the mortgage interest deduction.

Also, keep in mind that non-acquisition indebtedness cannot exceed the difference between the residence's fair market value and the amount of acquisition indebtedness.

The IRS defines points as any extra charges paid by a home buyer at closing in order to obtain a mortgage. In effect, points are prepaid interest. Points paid to secure a loan for the purchase, construction or improvement of a principal residence are usually fully deductible in the year you paid them. Points paid to refinance your home mortgage must be deducted ratably over the term of the loan.

After the home-mortgage interest deduction, the next most important tax break for homeowners is the deduction for real estate taxes. You can deduct real estate taxes and state and local property taxes on all your real estate. The only decision you may need to make is whether you prepay the coming year's taxes or delay the current year's taxes to see which way it might benefit you.

New Energy Incentives

For 2010, under the Non-business Energy Property Credit, you may be able to claim a credit of 30% of the costs of qualified energy-efficient property or improvements (residential energy property credit) and a 30% credit for solar energy and fuel-cell power plants (residential alternative energy credit). The credit, which was not available in 2008, has been reinstated and is available in 2010.

Beginning in 2010, the amount of the Non-Business Energy Property Credit that may be claimed cannot exceed the excess of the sum of the taxpayer's regular tax liability and the AMT liability over the sum of the non-refundable personal credits other than this credit and the foreign tax credit. Any unused credit amount for tax years in which these limits apply may be carried forward indefinitely.

Improvements include insulated walls or ceilings, energy-efficient exterior doors and windows, including skylights; specially treated metal roofs; and a high-efficiency furnace, air conditioner or water heater. The improvements must have been made in your principal residence located in the United States and the maximum credit is $1,500.

For 2010, under the Residential Energy Efficient Property Credit, there is no limitation on the credit amount for qualified solar electric property costs, qualified solar water-heating property costs, qualified small-wind energy property costs and qualified geothermal heat-pump property costs. The limitation on the credit amount for qualified fuel-cell property costs remains the same.

For property placed in service during 2011, an individual is entitled to a credit against tax in an amount equal to 10 percent of the amount paid for qualified energy efficiency improvements, and the amount of residential energy expenditures paid during the tax year.

The maximum credit allowable is $500 over the lifetime of the taxpayer. Energy efficient property must meet the criteria and certain residential energy property expenditures have credit limitations.

Home Office Deduction

With technology making it easier than ever for people to operate a business out of their home, many taxpayers may be able to take a home office deduction.

Here are five key points you should know about the home office deduction.

1. Generally, in order to claim a business deduction for your home office, you must use part of your home <u>exclusively and regularly</u>:

   - As your principal place of business, or
   - As a place to meet or deal with patients, clients or customers in the normal course of your business, or
   - In the case of a separate structure which is not attached to your home, it must be used in connection with your trade or business

   For certain storage use, rental use or daycare facility use, you are required to use the property regularly but not exclusively.

2. Generally, the amount you can deduct depends on the percentage of your home that you used for business. Your deduction for certain expenses will be limited if your gross income from your business is less than your total business expenses.
3. There are special rules for qualified daycare providers and for persons storing business inventory or product samples.
4. If you are self-employed, use Form 8829, Expenses for Business Use of Your Home, to figure your home office deduction then report the deduction on line 30 of Schedule C, Form 1040.
5. Different rules apply to claiming the home office deduction if you are an employee. For example, the regular and exclusive business use must be for the convenience of your employer.

Selling Your Home

For many years, the income tax rule for profits earned on the sale of a house has been favorable for those who sold their primary residence. The income tax rule in effect through December 31, 2008 was a homeowner who sold a house could exclude up to $250,000 (or up to $500,000 for married couples filing jointly) in profit from their taxes if the property was considered their primary residence. For a home to be considered the primary residence the taxpayer was required to live in the house for at least two years out of the five years ending on the date of sale. The use of the residence for the other three years did not affect the exclusion rule, with the exception of depreciation.

One part of the Housing Assistance Tax Act of 2008 changed this rule. Beginning January 1, 2009, the amount of profit from the sale of a house that can be excluded is now based on the percentage of time the house was used as a primary residence. If the house is used for anything other than primary residence, profits must be allocated between qualifying and non-qualifying use. Any non-qualifying use can possibly reduce the amount of profit that can be excluded. Non-qualifying uses are second homes, vacation homes, and rental properties.

Starting January 1, 2009, taxpayers planning to sell a non-qualifying property may want to move in and make the property their primary residence to gain as much qualifying use as possible before selling.

Lost Your Job

Getting laid off is scary, especially if you have a spouse and kids. It's important to know how to manage your money in that situation.

Unemployment compensation is taxable
A severance package counts as taxable income, including any money you get paid for accumulated vacation or sick time. Unlike wages, no tax is withheld from unemployment pay. So make sure to hold back about a quarter of that money for taxes.

In 2010 and 2011, the first $2,400 of unemployment compensation you received is excluded from your gross income and not subject to tax.

COBRA Premium Assistance

If you are laid off from a job where you received employer-provided health insurance, a federal law known as COBRA has allowed you to continue your health insurance coverage so long as you paid the full premium, plus any administrative fees. Many employees, especially after losing their jobs, found their ability to pay these premiums reduced and many had to give up the health coverage they enjoyed as an employee.

Starting in 2009, the federal government is subsidizing 65% of COBRA premiums for employees who were involuntarily terminated between September 1, 2008 and February 28, 2010. The assistance program is available for 15 months. The premium subsidy is in effect for any premium for a period of coverage beginning on or after February 17, 2009. If you are laid off, your employer should notify you about this rule.

The subsidy's tax-free element is reduced for singles with modified AGI between $125,000 and $145,000, and joint filers with modified AGI between $250,000 and $290,000. For singles with modified AGI above $145,000 and joint filers with modified AGI above $290,000, the subsidy is treated as gross income.

However, keep in mind that there may be less expensive approaches to healthcare coverage that should also be considered, such as those available to you through your spouse's plan or your professional association or union.

Mortgage Debt Cancellation

The last few years have created financial difficulties for many families, and this has led to a historic level of home foreclosures. In many cases, the sale of a foreclosed house does not yield enough money to pay off the mortgage. Prior to 2008, any debt forgiven by the mortgage holder would generally result in ordinary income to the borrower.

However, relief is now available in these circumstances. For debt discharged on or after January 1, 2007, and before January 1, 2013, the debt forgiveness is treated as tax free if the property is your primary residence. The limit on qualifying debt is $2 million ($1 million if married filing separately.)

This provision also applies where mortgage debt for a primary residence is forgiven as part of a refinance or other loan modification.

Alternative Motor Vehicle Credit

The Alternative Motor Vehicle Credit grants four separate credits for different types of energy-efficient vehicles. Your potential credit will be determined by the type of vehicle and which of the four credits apply.

One credit that is part of the Alternative Motor Vehicle Credit is the credit of up to $3,400 for hybrid vehicles. The credit is taken in the year you purchased the vehicle. However, the full credit only applies to the first 60,000 vehicles that the auto manufacturer sells. After that, the credit is phased-out. Ford has reached the limit, and no credit is available for any Ford or Mercury hybrid motor vehicle purchased after March 31, 2010. Honda has reached the limit, and no credit is available for any Honda hybrid motor vehicle purchased after December 31, 2008. Toyota has reached the limit, and no credit is available for any Toyota hybrid motor vehicle purchased after September 30, 2007. The credit is available for other automobile manufacturers.

New Qualified Plug-in Electric Drive Motor Vehicle
For qualified vehicles purchased in 2010, a plug-in electric drive motor vehicle credit is also available. For 2010, the credit is equal to $2,500 plus $417 for each kilowatt hour of traction battery capacity in excess of four kilowatt hours. The credit is capped at $7,500 for a vehicle with a gross weight of 14,000 pounds or less. The credit begins to phase out when the total number of qualified vehicles sold reaches 200,000.

Military Tax Tips

- **Moving Expenses**—If you are a member of the Armed Forces on active duty and you move because of a permanent change of station, you can deduct the reasonable unreimbursed expenses of moving you and members of your household.
- **Combat Pay**—If you serve in a combat zone as an enlisted person or as a warrant officer for any part of a month, all your military pay received for military service that month is not taxable. For officers, the monthly exclusion is capped at the highest enlisted pay, plus any hostile fire or imminent danger pay received.
- **Extension of Deadlines**—The time for taking care of certain tax matters can be postponed. The deadline for filing tax returns, paying taxes, filing claims for refund, and taking other actions with the IRS is automatically extended for qualifying members of the military.
- **Uniform Cost and Upkeep**—If military regulations prohibit you from wearing certain uniforms when off duty, you can deduct the cost and upkeep of those uniforms, but you must reduce your expenses by any allowance or reimbursement you receive.
- **Joint Returns**—Generally, joint returns must be signed by both spouses. However, when one spouse may not be available due to military duty, a power of attorney may be used to file a joint return.
- **Travel to Reserve Duty**—If you are a member of the US Armed Forces Reserves, you can deduct unreimbursed travel expenses for traveling more than 100 miles away from home to perform your reserve duties.
- **ROTC Students**—Subsistence allowances paid to ROTC students participating in advanced training are not taxable. However, active duty pay—such as pay received during summer advanced camp—is taxable.

- **Military Spouses**— For more than 60 years, service members have had the privilege of retaining residency in the same state regardless of where they were stationed. This means that service members pay income taxes to their home state, and they don't have to change their driver's license or vehicle and voters registration during each permanent change of station. Now, spouses have the same privileges. Under the old law, a service member's spouse had to change legal residence with every move. Now, the spouse can retain the same legal residence as the active-duty service member as long as they once shared that legal residency.
- **Transitioning Back to Civilian Life**—You may be able to deduct some costs you incur while looking for a new job. Expenses may include travel, resume preparation fees, and outplacement agency fees. Moving expenses may be deductible if your move is closely related to the start of work at a new job location, and you meet certain tests.

Ministers

If you are a minister, your earnings are subject to the self-employed tax unless you receive an exemption. If you are conscientiously opposed to public insurance because of your religious beliefs, then you can claim an exemption.

Remember, this exemption is permanent.

Death in the Family

It's sad but true: death doesn't stop the IRS. Laws exist to make sure your loved-one's taxable income, before his or her death, doesn't go untaxed. So, who files the taxes for your departed loved one? That responsibility falls to the executor of the estate or, if there is not an executor, a family member. The tax return is filled out the same way as if he or she was still alive, but "deceased" is written after the taxpayer's name.

A money inheritance from the death of a loved one is generally not subject to federal income tax. So, if your great aunt left you a sizeable certificate of deposit (C.D.), you don't have to pay taxes on it. However, once you own the inheritance, you must pay taxes on the interest it generates.

Things to Know If You Receive an IRS Notice

Every year, the IRS sends millions of letters and notices to taxpayers. Many taxpayers will receive this correspondence during the late summer and fall. Here are a few things every taxpayer should know about IRS notices—just in case one shows up in your mailbox.

1. Don't panic. Many of these letters can be dealt with simply and painlessly.
2. There are a number of reasons the IRS sends notices to taxpayers. The notice may request payment of taxes, notify you of a change to your account or request additional information. The notice you receive normally covers a very specific issue about your account or tax return.
3. Each letter and notice offers specific instructions on what you are asked to do to satisfy the inquiry.
4. If you receive a correction notice, you should review the correspondence and compare it with the information on your return.
5. If you agree with the correction to your account, usually no reply is necessary unless payment is due.
6. If you do not agree with the correction the IRS made, it is important that you respond as requested. Write to explain why you disagree. Include any documents and information you wish the IRS to consider, along with the bottom tear-off portion of the notice. Mail the information to the IRS address shown in the upper left-hand corner of the notice. Allow at least 30 days for a response.
7. Most correspondence can be handled without calling or visiting an IRS office. However, if you have questions, call the telephone number in the upper right-hand corner of the notice. Have a copy of your tax return and the correspondence available when you call to help respond to your inquiry.
8. Remember to always keep copies of your correspondence with your records.

Special Opportunity from
Richard A. Lindsey, CPA for the Readers of
"Crazy Little Shorts for These Taxing Times"

Dear Reader,

This can be the end or it can be a beginning. Hopefully you found value here and found me to be an interesting and engaging guy. Well, there's a lot more where this came from – and I'm confident enough to let you have a treasure trove of it for free, with the intent of you ultimately becoming a lifetime client.

So, I'd like you to sample my popular monthly newsletter, *Taxing Times...* pick my brain during monthly private, one-on-one telephone consultations or unlimited email queries... and pour over my highly acclaimed special report, The Top 10 Tax Mistakes the IRS Looks for and How to Avoid Them **all free.** (Just help us cover a small shipping/handling charge.)

Afterward, you can decide if you want your VIP Membership in Lindsey's Insider Circle to continue or not. It's a risk free test drive, and you'll score well over $300 in indispensable resources and strategies.

Right now, I invite you to activate your VIP Membership. **After your two month FREE test drive you will automatically continue at the <u>lowest</u> VIP Membership price of $19.95 per month. Should you decide to cancel your membership, you can do so at any time by calling Lindsey's Insider Circle at (251) 633-4070 or faxing a cancellation note to (251) 633-4071. Remember, your credit or debit card will NOT be charged the low monthly membership fee until the beginning of the 3rd month, which means** you will receive 2 one-on-one telephone consultations, the Special Report, 12 back issues and 2 full current issues of Taxing Times to read, digest and profit from all the powerful techniques and strategies you get from being an Insider Circle VIP Member. **And of course, it's impossible for you to**

lose, because if you don't absolutely LOVE everything you get, you can simply cancel your membership before the third month and never get billed a single penny for membership.

EMAIL REQUIRED IN ORDER TO NOTIFY YOU OF SPECIAL MEMBER ONLY CALL-IN TIMES

Name _____

Address _____

City _____ State _____ Zip _____

Email _____

Phone # 1 _____ Phone # 2 _____

Credit/Debit Card Instructions to Cover **$6.95** for Shipping & Handling

Card Number _____

Card Type _____ Exp Date _____

Credit Card Code (numbers on back of card) _____

Signature_____ Date _____

**Photocopy and Fax to:
(251) 633-4071**

**Or mail to:
1050 Hillcrest Rd., Ste A
Mobile, AL 36695**